SCHIRMER'S LIBRARY
OF MUSICAL CLASSICS

FREDERIC CHOPIN
Complete Works for the Piano

Edited and Fingered,
and provided with an Introductory Note by
CARL MIKULI

Historical and Analytical Comments by
JAMES HUNEKER

G. SCHIRMER, Inc.

DISTRIBUTED BY
HAL•LEONARD®
CORPORATION
7777 W. BLUEMOUND RD. P.O. BOX 13819 MILWAUKEE, WI 53213

FRÉDÉRIC FRANÇOIS CHOPIN

According to a tradition—and, be it said, an erroneous one—Chopin's playing was like that of one dreaming rather than awake—scarcely audible in its continual *pianissimos* and *una cordas*, with feebly developed technique and quite lacking in confidence, or at least indistinct, and distorted out of all rhythmic form by an incessant *tempo rubato!* The effect of these notions could not be otherwise than very prejudicial to the interpretation of his works, even by the most able artists—in their very striving after truthfulness; besides, they are easily accounted for.

Chopin played rarely and always unwillingly in public; "exhibitions" of himself were totally repugnant to his nature. Long years of sickliness and nervous irritability did not always permit him the necessary repose, in the concert-hall, for displaying untrammeled the full wealth of his resources. In more familiar circles, too, he seldom played anything but his shorter pieces, or occasional fragments from the larger works. Small wonder, therefore, that Chopin the Pianist should fail of general recognition.

Yet Chopin possessed a highly developed technique, giving him complete mastery over the instrument. In all styles of touch the evenness of his scales and passages was unsurpassed—nay, fabulous; under his hands the pianoforte needed to envy neither the violin for its bow nor wind-instruments for the living breath. The tones melted one into the other with the liquid effect of beautiful song.

A genuine piano-hand, extremely flexible though not large, enabled him to play arpeggios of most widely dispersed harmonies and passages in wide stretches, which he brought into vogue as something never attempted before; and everything without the slightest apparent exertion, a pleasing freedom and lightness being a distinguishing characteristic of his style. At the same time, the tone which he could *draw out* of the instrument was prodigious, especially in the *cantabiles;* in this regard John Field alone could compare with him.

A lofty, virile energy lent imposing effect to suitable passages—an energy without roughness; on the other hand, he could carry away his hearers by the tenderness of his soulful delivery—a tenderness without affectation. But with all the warmth of his peculiarly ardent temperament, his playing was always within bounds, chaste, polished and at times even severely reserved.

In keeping time Chopin was inflexible, and many will be surprised to learn that the metronome never left his piano. Even in his oft-decried *tempo rubato* one hand—that having the accompaniment—always played on in strict time, while the other, singing the melody, either hesitating as if undecided, or, with increased animation, anticipating with a kind of impatient vehemence as if in passionate utterances, maintained the freedom of musical expression from the fetters of strict regularity.

Some information concerning Chopin the Teacher, even in the shape of a mere sketch, can hardly fail to interest many readers.

Far from regarding his work as a teacher, which his position as an artist and his social connections in Paris rendered difficult of avoidance, as a burdensome task, Chopin daily devoted his entire energies to it for several hours and with genuine delight. True, his demands on the talent and industry of the pupil were very great. There were often "de leçons orageuses" ("stormy lessons"), as they were called in school parlance, and many a fair eye wet with tears departed from the high altar of the Cité d'Orleans, rue St. Lazare, yet without the slightest resentment on that score against the dearly beloved master. For this same severity, so little prone to easy satisfaction, this feverish vehemence with which the master strove to raise his disciples to his own plane, this insistence on the repetition of a passage until it was understood, were a guaranty that he had the pupil's progress at heart. He would glow with a sacred zeal for art; every word from his lips was stimulating and inspiring. Single lessons often lasted literally for several hours in succession, until master and pupil were overcome by fatigue.

On beginning with a pupil, Chopin was chiefly anxious to do away with any stiffness in, or cramped, convulsive movement of, the hand, thereby obtaining the first requisite of a fine technique, "souplesse" (suppleness), and at the same time independence in the motion of the fingers. He was never tired of inculcating that such technical exercises are not merely mechanical, but claim the intelligence and entire will-power of the pupil; and, consequently, that a twentyfold or fortyfold repetition (still the lauded arcanum of so many schools) does no good whatever—not to mention the kind of practising advocated by Kalkbrenner, during which one may also occupy oneself with reading! He treated the various styles of touch very thoroughly, more especially the full-toned *legato.*

As gymnastic aids he recommended bending the wrist inward and outward, the repeated wrist-stroke, the pressing apart of the fingers—but all with an earnest warning against over-exertion. For scale-practice he required a very full tone, as *legato* as possible, at first very slowly and taking a quicker tempo only step by step, and playing with metronomic evenness. To facilitate the passing under of the thumb and passing over of the fingers, the hand was to be bent inward. The scales having many black keys (B major, F-sharp, D-flat) were studied first, C major, as the hardest, coming last. In like order he took up Clementi's Preludes and Exercises, a work which he highly valued on account of its utility. According to Chopin, evenness in scale-playing and arpeggios depends not only on the equality in the strength of the fingers obtained through five-finger exercises, and a perfect freedom of the thumb in passing under and over, but fore-mostly on the perfectly smooth and constant sideways movement of the hand (not *step* by *step*), letting the elbow hang down freely and loosely at all times. This movement he exemplified by a *glissando* across the keys. After this he gave as studies a selection from Cramer's Études, Clementi's Gradus ad Parnassum, The Finishing Studies in Style by Moscheles, which were very congenial to him, Bach's English and French Suites, and some Preludes and Fugues from the Well-Tempered Clavichord.

Field's and his own nocturnes also figured to a certain extent as studies, for through them—partly by learning from his explanations, partly by hearing and imitating them as played indefatigably by Chopin himself—the pupil was taught to recognize, love and produce the *legato* and the beautiful connected singing tone. For paired notes and chords he exacted strictly simultaneous striking of the notes, an arpeggio being permitted only where marked by the composer himself; in the trill, which he generally commenced on the auxiliary, he required perfect evenness rather than great rapidity, the closing turn to be played easily and without haste.

For the turn (*gruppetto*) and appoggiatura he recommended the great Italian singers as models; he desired octaves to be played with the wrist-stroke, but without losing in fullness of tone thereby. Only far-advanced pupils were given his Études Op. 10 and Op. 25.

Chopin's attention was always directed to teaching correct phrasing. With reference to wrong phrasing he often repeated the apt remark, that it struck him as if some one were reciting, in a language not understood by the speaker, a speech carefully learned by rote, in the course of which the speaker not only neglected the natural quantity of the syllables, but even stopped in the middle of words. The pseudo-musician, he said, shows in a similar way, by his wrong phrasing, that music is not his mother-tongue, but something foreign and incomprehensible to him, and must, like the aforesaid speaker, quite renounce the idea of making any effect upon his hearers by his delivery.

In marking the fingering, especially that peculiar to himself, Chopin was not sparing. Piano-playing owes him many innovations in this respect, whose practicalness caused their speedy adoption, though at first certain authorities, like Kalkbrenner, were fairly horrified by them. For example, Chopin did not hesitate to use the thumb on the black keys, or to pass it under the little finger (with a decided inward bend of the wrist, to be sure), where it facilitated the execution, rendering the latter quieter and smoother. With one and the same finger he often struck two neighboring keys in succession (and this not simply in a slide from a black key to the next white one), without the slightest noticeable break in the continuity of the tones. He frequently passed the longest fingers over each other without the intervention of the thumb (see Étude No. 2, Op. 10), and not only in passages where (e.g.) it was made necessary by the holding down of a key with the thumb. The fingering for chromatic thirds based on this device (and marked by himself in Étude No. 5, Op. 25), renders it far easier to obtain the smoothest *legato* in the most rapid tempo, and with a perfectly quiet hand, than the fingering followed before. The fingerings in the present edition are, in most cases, those indicated by Chopin himself; where this is not the case, they are at least marked in conformity with his principles, and therefore calculated to facilitate the execution in accordance with his conceptions.

In the shading he insisted on a real and carefully graduated *crescendo* and *decrescendo*. On phrasing, and on style in general, he gave his pupils invaluable and highly suggestive hints and instructions, assuring himself, however, that they were understood by playing not only single passages, but whole pieces, over and over again, and this with a scrupulous care, an enthusiasm, such as none of his auditors in the concert-hall ever had an opportunity to witness. The whole lesson-hour often passed without the pupil's having played more than a few measures, while Chopin, at a Pleyel upright piano (the pupil always played on a fine concert grand, and was obliged to promise to practise on only the best instruments), continually interrupting and correcting, proffered for his admiration and imitation the warm, living ideal of perfect beauty. It may be asserted, without exaggeration, that only the pupil knew Chopin the Pianist in his entire unrivalled greatness.

Chopin most urgently recommended ensemble-playing, the cultivation of the best chamber-music—but only in association with the finest musicians. In case no such opportunity offered, the best substitute would be found in four-hand playing.

With equal insistence he advised his pupils to take up thorough theoretical studies as early as practicable. Whatever their condition in life, the master's great heart always beat warmly for the pupils. A sympathetic, fatherly friend, he inspired them to unwearying endeavor, took unaffected delight in their progress, and at all times had an encouraging word for the wavering and dispirited.

CARL MIKULI.

FOUR SCHERZI AND FANTASY

FRÉDÉRIC Chopin bequeathed to the world of music six solo Scherzi. The four that comprise a group are opus 20, in B minor, published February, 1835; opus 31, in B flat minor, published December, 1837; opus 39, in C sharp minor, published October, 1840; and opus 54, in E major, published December, 1843. The remaining two Scherzi are to be found in his second Sonata, opus 35, and third Sonata, opus 58, and are discussed in the volume devoted to the Three Sonatas. These six compositions are most striking evidences of Chopin's originality, power and delicacy. The Scherzo, however, is not his invention. Beethoven and Mendelssohn anticipated him. But he took the form, remodelled and filled it with a surprisingly novel content, though not altering its three-four measure. In Beethoven we feel the humor of his Scherzo, its swing, its robustness, its rude jollity. One enjoys the lightness, velocity and finish of Mendelssohn's *scherzando* moods; strictly speaking, they contain more of the true Scherzo idea than Chopin's. Mendelssohn's sentiment of refined joyousness stems from Scarlatti and other early Italian masters of the piano. They are full of a certain gracious life, a surface-skimming of sentiment like the curved flight of birds over shallow waters. But we enter a different, a terrible, a beautiful domain in the Chopin Scherzi. Two only have the clarity of atmosphere, lightness of touch, and sweet gayety of the veritable Scherzo; the others are grave, fierce, sardonic, demoniacal, ironic, passionate, hysterical and most melancholy. In some the mood seems pathologic; in some enigmatic; in all the mood is magical. These four Scherzi are psychical records, confessions committed to paper of outpourings that never could have passed the lips. From these we may reconstruct the inner Chopin, whose well-bred exterior so ill prepared the world for the tragic issues of his music.

The first Scherzo in B minor is in his most sombre, ironic and reckless vein; Chopin throwing himself to the very winds of remorse. A self-torturing, a Manfred mood. Structurally speaking it is a fair model for the others: a few bars of introduction—the porch, as Niecks would call it—a principal subject, a trio, a short working-out section, a skillful return to the opening theme and an elaborate *coda*. Some pianists play the piece without the repeats and it is the gainer thereby, as the *da capo* is unsuited to latter-day taste. The architecture, not technically flawless, is better adapted to the florid musical beauties of the Byzantine than to the severer Hellenic line. The arabesque-like figure after the eight-bar introduction—muted bars some of them, as is Chopin's wont—bears a certain spiritual likeness to the principal figure in the Fantaisie-Impromptu. But instead of the ductile triplets, as in the bass of the Impromptu, the figure in the Scherzo is divided between two hands, and the harshness of the mood is emphasized by the anticipatory chord in the left hand. The vitality of the first page is remarkable. The questioning chords at the close of the section are as imaginative as any Chopin wrote. The half-notes and up-leaping *appoggiatura* testify to his originality in details; these occur before the modulation into the lyric theme in B, and with a slight change at the dash into the *coda*. The second section, *agitato*, contains some knotty harmonic problems; it must be taken at a tempestuous speed, else cacophony. Chopin here is bold to excess. The *molto più lento* is a masterpiece; it is written in the luscious key of B major and is a woven tonal enchantment. It is only comparable to the B major episode in the B minor Étude for octaves, or to the Tuberose Nocturne in B major. Mark how the composer returns to his first savage mood. It is a picture of contrasted violence. The *coda* is like an electrifying cross-country ride, barbaric in its impetuosity. The heavy accentuation on the first note of every bar should not blind one's rhythmic sense to the second beat in the left hand, which is likewise accented. These mixed rhythms add to the general despair of the *finale*. The shrill dissonances, so logical, so effective, must have lacerated the eardrums of Chopin's contemporaries. And they must be vigorously insisted upon. I think it was Tausig who first taught his pupils to use the interlocked octaves at the close instead of the chromatic scales in unison, though I suppose Liszt did it before any one else; he always thought of such things, even when the composer did not. Chopin, however, probably objected to the innovation, which may be admissible. Coming after the Hercules-vein of the *coda* the plain scales sound a trifle thin and tame. This Scherzo has been criticised as being too much in the étude style, but that depends very much upon the pianist who plays it. When Rubinstein sat in front of the keyboard it became in his hands a tornado of wrathful mutterings and outcries. It was his favorite.

We are on more familiar footing in the second Scherzo in B flat minor. Who has not heard with a certain awe those arched questioning triplets, which Chopin never could get his pupils to play sufficiently *tombé!* "It must be a charnel-house," he told De Lenz. But those vaulted phrases have since become banal. Alas! This Scherzo, like the lovely A flat Ballade, has been done to death. Yet, how fresh, how vigorous, how abounding in sweetness and light is this music when it falls from the hands of a master. It is then a Byronic poem, "So tender, so bold, so full of love, as of scorn"—to quote Schumann. Chopin never penned a more delicious song than the trio. The section in A is serious to severity, yet how penetrating is its perfume. The excursion into C sharp minor may be the awakening of the wondering dream; but it is balanced, with no suggestions of the pallid morbidities of the other Chopin. Style and theme are perfectly welded. It all lies in the very heart of the piano. Fearful that he has dwelt too long upon the idea, the composer breaks away and follows a burst into the clear sky. After the repetition comes the working-out section, and though ingenious and effective, it is always in development that Chopin is weakest. The Olympian aloofness of Beethoven he has not; he cannot survey his material from an objective viewpoint. He is a great composer, but he is also a great pianist. He nursed his ideas with constructive frugality, but the instrument often checked his imagination. There is logic in the exposition of this Scherzo, but it is piano-logic, not always music-logic. A certain straining after brilliancy, a falling off in the spontaneous urge of the early pages force us to feel happier when the first triplet figure returns. The *coda* is strong. This Scherzo will remain the favored one. It is not cryptic or repellent like the two examples in B minor and C sharp minor, and therefore is a perennial joy to pupil, teacher and public. Yet it is not as logical, as profound, as the first and third Scherzi.

The third Scherzo in C sharp minor was composed, or else finished, at Majorca. It is the most dramatic of this set. Irony lurks in its polished phrases and there is fever and seething scorn. The work is clear-cut and of exact balance. Chopin founded whole paragraphs either on a single phrase repeated in similar shapes or on two phrases in alternation—a primitive practice in Polish folksong. Hadow asserts that "Beethoven does not attain the lucidity of his style by such parallelism of phraseology," and admits that Chopin's methods made for "clearness and precision . . . and may be regarded as a characteristic of the national manner." A thoroughly personal characteristic, too. There is virile clangor on the firmly struck octaves of the opening page—no hesitating, morbid view of life, but harsh assertiveness, not untinged with splenetic anger. The chorale of the trio is admirably devised and carried out, though its piety may well be a bit of liturgical make-believe. Here the contrasts are most artistic—sonorous harmonies set off by broken chords that deliciously tinkle. There is a frenetic *coda* and the close in the major

is surprising considering what has preceded it. Never to become the property of the profane, the C sharp minor Scherzo, notwithstanding its marked asperity of mood, is a supreme art in its particular province. Without the inner freedom of its predecessors, it is more self-contained than the B minor Scherzo. But it is a sombre and fantastic pile of architecture, and about it hovers despairing and perpetual night. It is a tale from Poe's "iron-bound, melancholy volume of the magi," and on its gates might be inscribed the word Spleen. De Lenz relates that Chopin dedicated the work to his pupil Gutmann, because this giant, with the fist of a prize-fighter, could "knock a hole in the table" with a certain chord for the left hand—sixth measure from the beginning—and adds quite naïvely: "Nothing more was ever heard of Gutmann—he was a discovery of Chopin's." Chopin died in this same Gutmann's arms, and, despite De Lenz, Gutmann was, until the death of the master, a "favorite pupil."

The fourth Scherzo in E may be described by no better word than delightful. It is sunny music, and its swiftness, sweep, and directness are compelling. The five preluding bars of half-notes, *unisono*, strike at once the keynote of optimism. What follows is like the ruffling of tree-tops by warm south winds. The upward little flight in E, beginning at the seventeenth bar, and in major thirds and fourths, has been happily utilized by Saint-Saëns in the Scherzo of his G minor piano concerto. The fanciful embroidery of the single finger passages is crystalline in clarity. A sparkling freedom and bubbling freshness characterize this Scherzo, too seldom heard in concert recitals. It is not in emotional content deep; it lies well within the categories of the capricious and elegant. On its fourth page it contains an episode in E which at first blush suggests the theme of the Waltz in A flat, opus 42, with its interminglements of duple and triple rhythms. The *più lento* further on has a touch of sadness; it is but the blur of a passing cloud that shadows with its fleecy edges the wind-swept moorland. The prevailing mood is one of joyousness; as joyous as the witty, sensitive Pole ever allowed himself to be. Its *coda* is not as forceful as the usual Chopin *coda*, and there is a dazzling flutter of silvery scale at the end. It is a charming work, a jesting of a superior sort. Niecks thinks it fragmentary. I find the fairy-like mood a relief after the doleful message of the earlier Scherzi. There is the same "spirit of opposition"; of sneering arrogance, none. Yet the composition seems to be banned by both classicists and Chopin-worshippers.

Robert Schumann, after remarking that the cosmopolitan must "sacrifice the small interests of the soil on which he was born," notes that the later works of Chopin "begin to lose something of their essential Sarmatian physiognomy, to approach partly the universal ideal cultivated by

the divine Greeks, which we find again in Mozart."
The F minor Fantasy, opus 49, has hardly the
Mozartian serenity, yet it parades a formal beauty,
not disfigured by excess of violence, either personal
or patriotic, and its melodies, though restless
and melancholy, are of surpassing nobility and
dramatic grandeur. I do not fear to maintain that
this Fantasy is one of the greatest among piano
pieces. After more than a half-century of neglect
it has at last been given its due position in the
pianists' pantheon. For Niecks, who did not at
first discern its worth, it suggests a Titan in com-
motion. It is titanic, the torso of some Faust-like
dream. It is Chopin's Faust. A *macabre* march,
containing some dangerous dissonances, gravely
ushers us to ascending staircases of triplets, only
to precipitate us into the very abysses of the piano
bass. The first subject, is is not as puissant and as
passionate as if Beethoven had written it? But
Chopin's lack of tenaciousness is soon apparent.
Beethoven would have built a tonal cathedral on
such a foundational scheme; but Chopin, ever
prodigal in his melody-making, impetuously dashes
on to the A flat episode, that heroic love-chant, so
often played with the effeminacies of the salon.
Its reappearance in various keys, the peaceful
Lento Sostenuto in B and conclusion are alike
masterly.

Vladimir de Pachmann avers that Franz Liszt
told him the programme of this Fantasy, according
to Chopin. At the close of one immemorial day the
composer was at the piano, his spirits vastly de-
pressed. Suddenly came a knocking at the door,
a Poe-like, sinister tapping which he at once rhyth-
mically echoed upon the keyboard. The first two
bars of the Fantasy describe these rappings, just as
the third and fourth stand for Chopin's musical in-
vitation, *entrez! entrez!* All this repeated till the
doors swinging wide admit George Sand, Liszt,
Madame Camille Pleyel (*née* Mock) and others of
the Chopin group. To the solemn measures of the
march they enter and range themselves about the
pianist, who, after the agitated triplets, begins his
complaint in the mysterious F minor song. But
Madame Sand, with whom he had quarrelled, falls
before him on her knees and pleads for pardon.
Straightway the chant merges into the appealing A
flat section, and from the C minor the current be-
comes more tempestuous until the climax is reached,
and to the second march (which for me always has a
Schumannesque tinge) the intruders rapidly vanish.
This far from ideal reading may be an authoritative
one, coming as it does from Chopin by way of
Liszt. I console myself for its rather commonplace
character with the notion that, perhaps, in its re-
telling, the story has caught some personal cadenzas
of the two historians.

Chopin had never before so artistically maintained
such an exalted passion, displayed such intellectual
power or kept to such a euphonious level, as in
the F minor Fantasy. It is his largest canvas, the
phraseology is broad and long-breathed, and there
is no padding of paragraphs. The virtuoso makes
way for the poet. The interest is not relaxed until
the final bar. This big work approaches Beethoven
in its unity, in theme, mood, formal rectitude
and economy of thematic material. I am loath to
believe that the echo of its magical music will ever
fall upon unheeding ears.

James Hunetker

Thematic Index.

Scherzos and Fantaisie.

SCHERZO.

a Mr. F. ALBRECHT.

Presto con fuoco. ($\textbf{.} = 120.$)

F. CHOPIN. Op. 20.

1.

Scherzo.

à Mlle la Comtesse de FÜRSTENSTEIN.

F. CHOPIN. Op. 31.

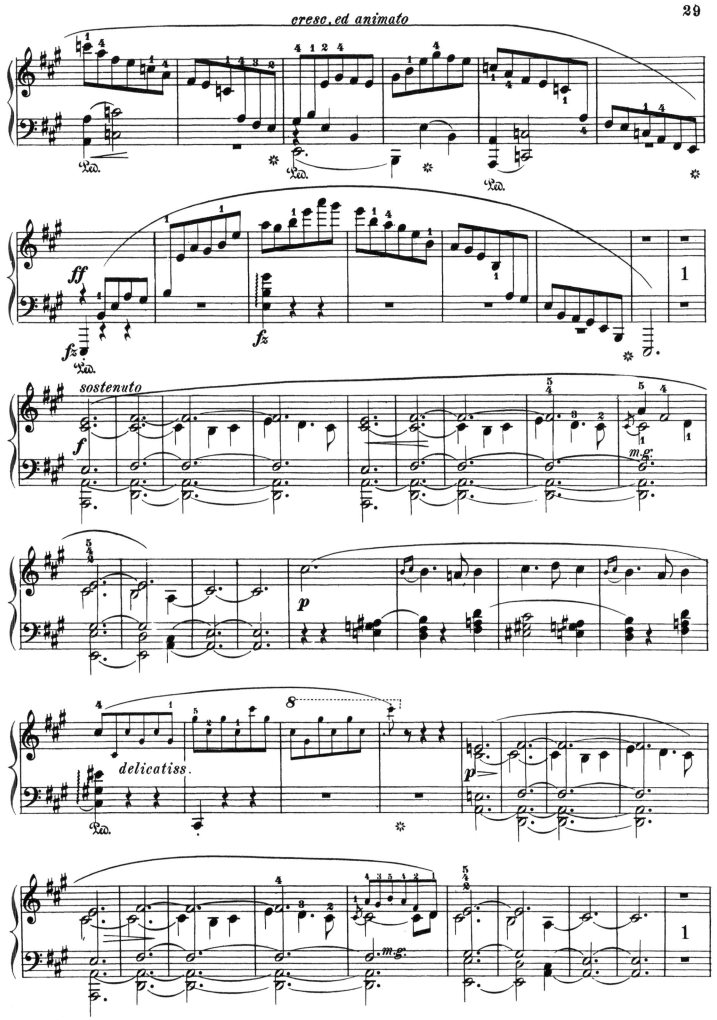

SCHERZO.

à Mr. A. GUTMAN.

F. CHOPIN, Op. 39.

Presto con fuoco.

SCHERZO.

à Mlle CLOTILDE de CARAMAN.

F. CHOPIN. Op. 54.

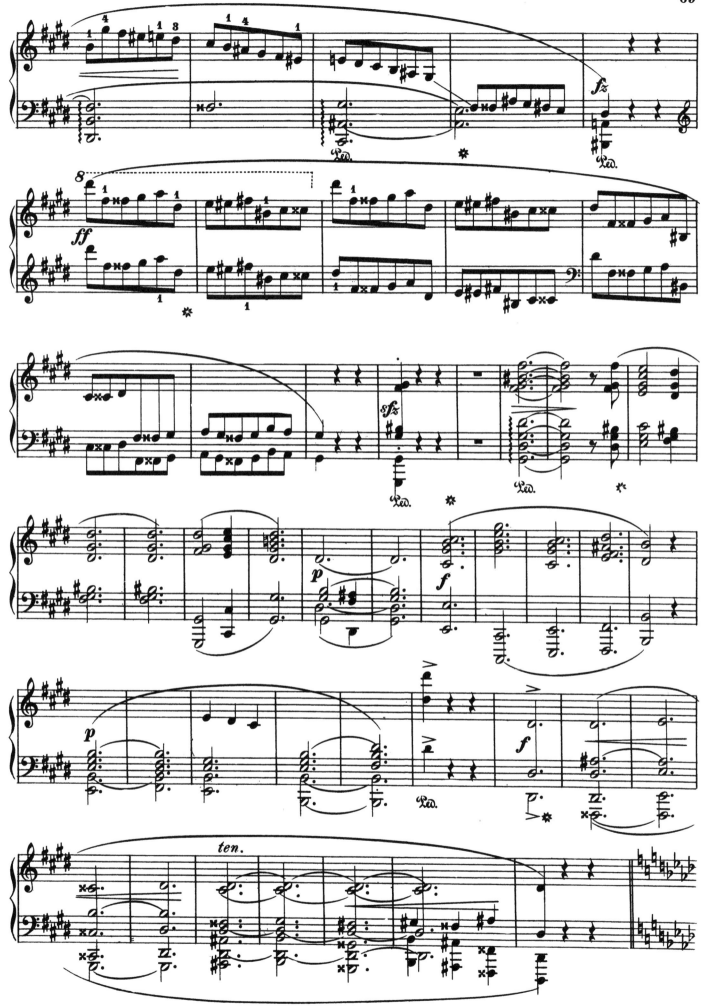

a tempo, ma poco a poco più presto.

FANTAISIE.

à Mme la Princesse CATH. de SOUZZO.

F. CHOPIN. Op. 49.

Tempo di marcia.

Adagio sostenuto.

Allegro assai.